Contents

KW-054-816

About Sorting Information

What can you say about the things around you? Loads! We spend lots of time describing things and asking about them.

The right question

To get and share useful **information**, we have to ask the right questions. Imagine you've lost your ball.

Your friend asks you 'which ball?' You could say 'my favourite one'.

Unless they know your favourite, this won't help to find it.

Let's Start! ICT →

Sorting Information

JERSEY LIBRARY	
JE 5OO5157 1	
Askews	2006
005.74	£5.99

Anne Rooney

QED Publishing

JE 5005157 1

Copyright © QED Publishing 2005

First published in the UK in 2005 by
QED Publishing
A Quarto Group Company
226 City Road
London EC1V 2TT

www.qed-publishing.co.uk

All rights reserved. No part of this publication
may be reproduced, stored in a retrieval system,
or transmitted in any form or by any means,
electronic, mechanical, photocopying, recording,
or otherwise, without the prior permission of the
publisher, nor be otherwise circulated in any form
of binding or cover other than that in which it is
published and without a similar condition being
imposed on the subsequent purchaser.

A Catalogue record for this book is available from
the British Library.

ISBN 1 84538 422 9

Written by Anne Rooney
Consultant: Philip Stubbs
Designed by Jacqueline Palmer
Editor: Louisa Somerville
Illustrator: John Haslam
Photographer: Ray Moller
Models provided by Scallywags

Publisher: Steve Evans
Creative Director: Louise Morley
Editorial Manager: Jean Coppendale

Anne Rooney has asserted her right under the
Copyright, Designs and Patents Act 1988 to be
identified as the author of this work.

Printed and bound in China

Words in bold **like this** are explained in the Glossary on page 30.

It would be better to say 'the red one with yellow spots' or 'the white one with blue spots'.
Now your friend can help you look for it!

This book shows you how to ask the right questions to find out about something. Computers help us to work with the information we find out.

All the same?

We can say how things are the same. We can also say how they are different. Things can be the same or different in lots of ways.

My flowers are all different colours.

The same or different?

In one way, the things below are all the same. They're all red.

In some ways, the things are different. Only the apple is a fruit. Only the car is made of metal. Only the fish can swim.

Look carefully

Sometimes, things that look quite different are also the same in some ways.

What's the same about all of these?

These things are different colours and shapes. What makes them the same is that they are all fruit.

7

Spot the difference!

How easy is it to spot differences between things?

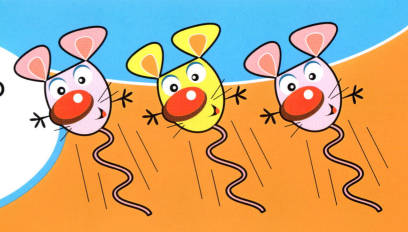

Easy peasy!

It's easy to spot the difference when things are the same shape but different colours.

It's also easy to spot when things are the same colour but different shapes.

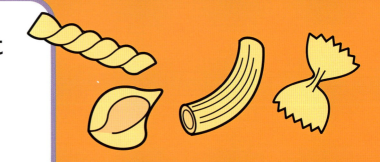

Odd one out

It's harder when things look similar. In an odd-one-out puzzle, you have to work out what makes one thing different from the others.

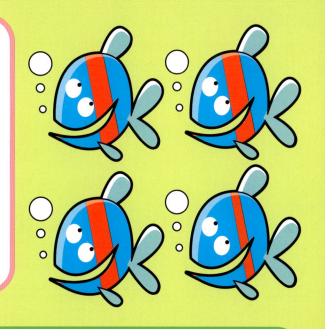

You might have played spot-the-difference puzzles, too. You look at pictures that are nearly the same and spot the things that are different.

Can you spot five differences between these two pictures?

green hat on clown, smaller red nose, yellow ball missing, clown's arm missing, patch on dog's eye

Asking questions

One way to help you tell things apart is to ask questions about them. You can find out how they are the same and how they are different.

Types of answers

Some types of questions need an answer 'yes' or 'no'. If someone asks, 'Do your shoes have laces?' the answer would be either 'yes' or 'no'.

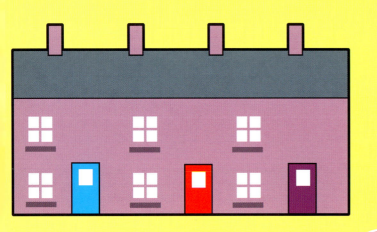

Some questions have other words as the answer. If someone asked, 'What colour is your front door?' the answer might be 'blue' or 'red' or 'purple'.

10

Other questions have numbers as the answer. If someone asked, 'How many sisters do you have?' the answer would be a number.

The answer could be one, two, three, or more. If you have no sisters, it would be zero.

How many answers?

Often, there is only one correct answer to a question.

What colour is your hair?

brown

red

blonde

black ✓

Which smells do you like?

toast ✓

roses

fish fingers

wet dog ✓

toothpaste ✓

Some questions let you give more than one answer.

Describing things

If someone asks you what something is like, you need to describe it to them. A description tells us about something.

Questions and answers

To find out about something, you can ask questions. If your friend told you they had a new jumper, you might ask:

'What colour is it?'
'Blue.'

'What's the pattern like?'
'Yellow spots.'

'Does it have a zip?'
'Yes.'

Making a description

You can put together words that tell you about things to make a description.

Imagine your friend says to you, 'What's your new toy like?'

You could answer by giving a description:

'It's a big purple, furry monster.'

It's got yellow horns and an orange nose.

Practise!

Play this game with a friend. Think of an animal and say three things to describe it – but don't name it.

For example, you could say, 'It's long and slippery and hisses.' Your friend has to guess that it's a snake – the fewer guesses the better!

Useful questions

Some questions and some answers are more useful than others.

Ask the right question

To find out about something, you need to ask useful questions.

I've lost my bag.

What colour is it?

This is a useful question. It will help you to look for the bag.

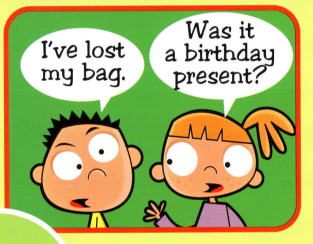

I've lost my bag.

Was it a birthday present?

This isn't a helpful question.

It's information about the bag, but it doesn't tell you what to look for.

Be exact

Ask your question in a way that will get the most useful answer. Questions such as, 'What's it like?' could have lots of different answers.

Think about the information that will be useful. What do you need to know?

What does it eat?

What's its name?

Which child's question is helpful for looking after the fish?

Yes or no?

When you're working with information in class or on the computer, questions with a small choice of answers are the most useful.

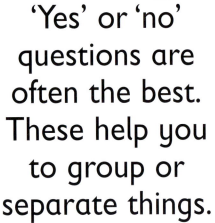

'Yes' or 'no' questions are often the best. These help you to group or separate things.

Use a tree!

A **tree diagram** can help you work out what things are. At each branch, you answer a question, then follow the right path.

Answer each question in turn. In the end, you will get to the answers!

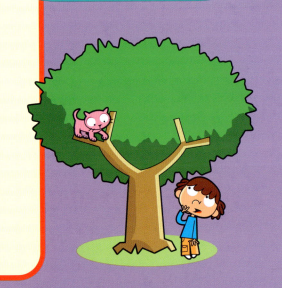

By asking and answering the questions in turn, you can work out what each **minibeast** is.

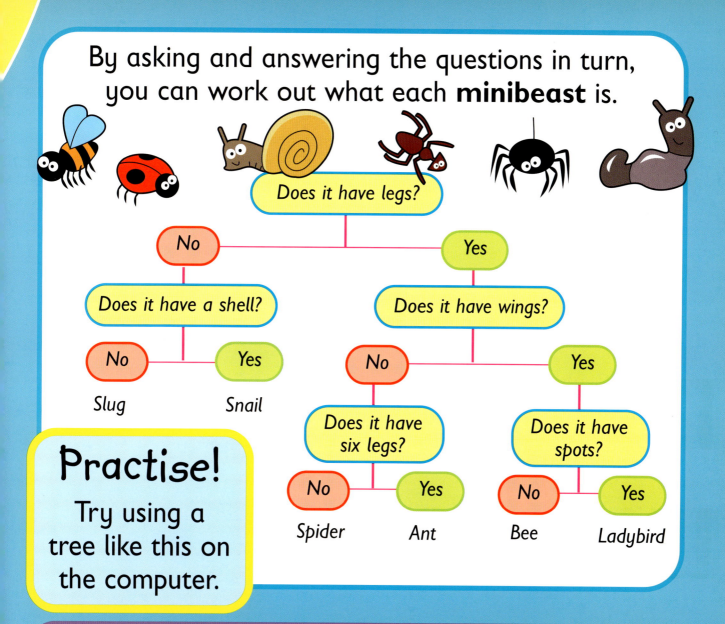

Does it have legs?

No

Yes

Does it have a shell?

Does it have wings?

No

Yes

No

Yes

Slug

Snail

Does it have six legs?

Does it have spots?

No

Yes

No

Yes

Spider

Ant

Bee

Ladybird

Practise!

Try using a tree like this on the computer.

Yes or no game

- Ask a friend to think of a sport.

- Ask your friend questions with a 'yes' or 'no' answer. You might say, 'Is it played with a ball?'. You can't ask, 'How many players?' because that doesn't have a 'yes' or 'no' answer.

- Can you name the sport in under 10 questions?

Making sets

When you ask the right questions about things, you can start to group them into **sets**.

This means putting things that are similar together.

What colour?

If you had a set of wooden blocks like these, you could divide them into sets of different colours.

You would have a set of red blocks, a set of blue blocks and a set of green blocks.

The sets may not be the same size. There might be more green blocks than blue blocks or red blocks.

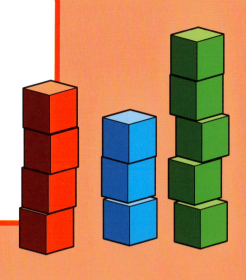

Other sets

Think of other ways of dividing things into sets.

You could group paintbrushes by how big they are.

You could group children into boys and girls.

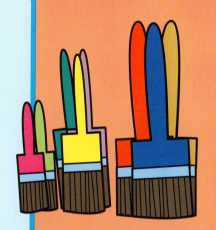

Which set?

Children aren't only boys or girls. They are also tall or short, and have curly or straight hair. Things can be grouped in different ways.

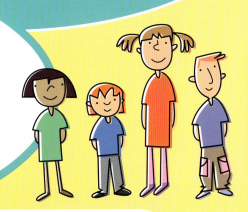

Making more sets

Imagine you had blocks like these.

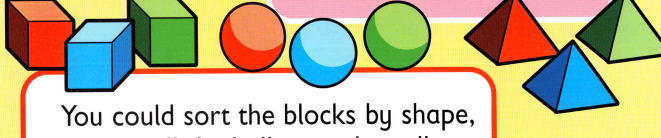

You could sort the blocks by shape, putting all the balls together, all the cubes together and all the **pyramids** together.

Or you could sort them by colour, making a red set, a blue set and a green set.

If someone chose one of these blocks, you could find out which one by asking two questions:

'What colour is it?'
'What shape is it?'

Practise!

Divide something in the classroom into sets. You might use pencils, or a shoe from each of your friends. How many ways can you divide them into sets?

You could separate pencils with rubbers from those without rubbers.

You could divide shoes by colour.

Making charts

You can ask questions to find out information to make a chart. You might ask people which type of film they like best.

People could tick the type of film they like on a question sheet.

Which sort of film do you like? Tick each type you like to watch.
Cartoons /////
Adventures ////
Fairy tales //
Space films //
Funny films ////

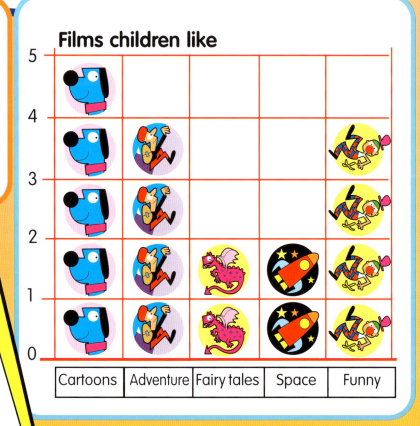

Films children like

	Cartoons	Adventure	Fairy tales	Space	Funny

When you make the chart, you see that two people like space films and four like funny films.

Does anyone like both space films and funny films? Your chart doesn't tell you.

Can you tell who likes adventure films?

Can you tell if anyone likes films about animals?

Can you tell if anyone does not like films at all?

The chart tells you about how many people like each type of film. But that's all. There's lots the chart does not tell you.

Keeping information

You can use a computer to keep track of lots of information and to work things out from the information.

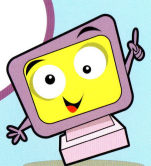

Databases

A **program** for keeping information is called a **database**. In a database, you could keep a list of people and the types of film they like.

You could search your database to find out information such as:

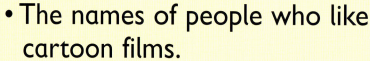

- The names of people who like cartoon films.
- Who likes cartoons and space films.
- Which people don't like any of these types of film.

Name: Nazeem Kahn

Cartoons ☑ Space film ☑
Adventure ☐ Funny film ☑
Fairy tale ☐

Name: Jemma Brown

Cartoons ☐ Space film ☑
Adventure ☑ Funny film ☑
Fairy tale ☐

You could still get the information to make a chart showing how many people like each kind of film. The database would probably even draw it for you!

I don't know!

A database can only tell you information that you've put in. The films database could tell you who likes adventure films.

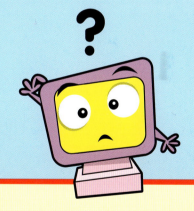

But it couldn't tell you the name of someone's favourite film, unless you had put this in.

Over to you

Now it's time to do some work of your own.

Guess who?

Play a game to help you practise asking 'yes' or 'no' questions and practise putting things into groups.

You'll need to play with your whole class. Everyone stands up. One person picks someone in the class, but they mustn't say who it is.

Take it in turns to ask a yes or no question to try to work out who it is. If someone says, 'Is it a boy?' and the answer is 'yes', all the girls have to sit down.

Keep asking questions until only one person is left.

With a bit of help

Make a question sheet and enter information about the people in your class.

Ask your teacher to help you put the information into a database on the computer.

By asking questions to **search** the database, you can find, for example, all the people with black hair and glasses, or all the people with blue eyes and short hair.

The same and different

Find out how many ways you can divide some objects into sets. If you play this with a friend, you can take it in turns to collect objects.

Finding things

Collect together lots of things, either at home or in the classroom.

These are the things you will divide into sets. If you're playing with a friend, you can collect objects for each other.

What's the same?

Try to find some things that are the same about some of your objects.

Are they the same shape? The same colour? Used for the same thing? Made of the same material?

Divide your objects into different sets.

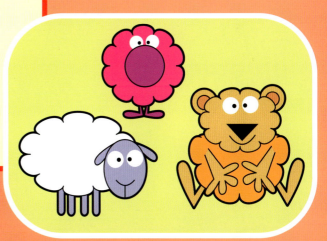

All about…

Describe one of your things, without saying what it is. Your friend has to work out from the description which thing you are talking about.

Glossary

database   Collection of facts about things kept on the computer.

information   Facts or details.

minibeast   Small animal, such as a spider, snail or beetle.

program   Set of instructions for a computer to follow.

pyramid   3-D shape with a triangular or square base and three or four triangular sides that meet at a point.

search   Use a computer to find information.

set   Group of things that are similar in some way.

tree diagram   Lines making a branching tree, with questions to help you make choices or work out what something is.

Index

Grown-up zone

Sorting Information
and the National Curriculum

The work in this book will help children to cover the following parts of the National Curriculum ICT scheme of work: unit 1d, unit 2e.

It can be tied in with work on science, design and technology and any other area of the curriculum in which the children can think about grouping and classifying objects or information.

Encourage children to work together and discuss how to classify objects in ways that are clear and useful. Encourage them to find features that will help divide objects into groups, and to identify single objects. Try to make sure early sorting produces groups, so that these can be subdivided. It's less useful to isolate individual objects from the start.

Children should be encouraged to review, evaluate and improve their own work at all stages. When working with databases, ask them to classify new objects using the ways they have developed.